LOREN GOES EXPLORING

THE APE CAVE

ADVENTURE

LOREN AND HIS DAD ARE OFF TO EXPLORE A LAVA TUBE CAVE. LOREN WILL CONFRONT HIS FEAR OF THE DARK. A FEAR THAT WE ALL HAVE WHEN WE ARE SMALL.

WRITTEN BY

JEFF KLINGER

The morning sunlight enters our windows to wake us. Its light pushes back the glow from Loren's night light to a small corner of his bedroom. I turn off the small light that helps keep his fear of the dark under control. A fear that we all have at 5 years old.

After the rainy days and grey clouds of spring, the clear blue sky and sunshine looks wonderful!
"Time to get up sleepy!" I tell him.

3

"What should we do on such a beautiful Saturday?" I ask him.
I remember we have been talking about exploring the lava tube caves, near Mount Saint Helens, called Ape Caves.
"Do you want to explore a cave?" I ask him.
Excitement lights up Loren's face.
"Yes! I want to explore a cave!"

The only thing I wonder about is Loren's fear of the dark.

Driving out of downtown Tacoma, we find ourselves in very slow traffic. Several lanes are shut down for repairs and causing delays. I say to Loren, "this is not cool."
Loren agrees, "this is not cool!"

Reprograming the GPS, we leave the tangle of traffic behind to continue driving on back roads. We are now making good time.

Driving down the winding back roads, we are passing through the scenic foothills of Mount Rainier. We see many small farms among the trees and hills. Some are set against the backdrop of Mount Rainer. Many appear suddenly as we pass by thick growths of evergreen trees.

We pass by fields with cows
grazing. Some look at us driving
by but most keep on eating and
pay no attention to us.

We are surprised to see fields
with llamas. They seem to be
paying more attention to us than
the cows. Maybe because they
are more of a pet than a farm
animal, like the cows are, and are
friendly with people.

In some fields, farmers are planting and cultivating crops.

All the things we see remind us there is another world outside the city that we rarely visit. I'm now glad the road repairs made us take the less traveled roads.

15

Rounding a curve in the road,
an orange sign greets us saying
"road closed ahead." Not long
after I see a brown sign for
Layser Cave near the entrance to
a gravel road.
Driving a little further we reach a
barrier across the road. Having
no alternative, we reluctantly turn
around and head back to travel
the major roads.

ROAD
CLOSED

The sign for Layser Cave greets us again.

I tell Loren, "our closed road may not have been a total waste. Let's see what this cave looks like."

"This doesn't look too promising," I think. But we need a break from riding in the car anyway and get out to stretch our legs.

"Let's go check out the cave." I say to Loren. And we are soon walking down the trail and into the woods.

The sun now shines directly overhead, making the forest bright and warm. A light breeze feels wonderful on our skin. We hear the leaves rustling softly, as their shadows sway across the trail in front of us.

Carefully making our way down the steep trail, it levels out and we come to a fork. Looking beyond the left branch, we see a wood platform and head that way. From the platform, we find ourselves overlooking a beautiful valley!

20

A natural viewpoint, long before the platform was built over it, it's easy to imagine it being used by natives to look for deer. Or maybe they used it to keep a lookout for visitors. Then again, they could have come to enjoy the wonderful view and warm themselves in the sun, as we are. Pulling ourselves away from the view, we retrace our steps to the trails fork and take the right branch.

Following the trail along the hillside, we walk around a large rock outcrop and find ourselves at the entrance to Layser Cave. A natural rock formation, the cave is perfect for shelter and was used by natives for about 6,000 years.

Entering the cave, we look up and see the roof is blackened from generations of fires used for warmth and cooking. The floor is cluttered with the remains of more recent fires.

Loren explores the cave, smiling and talking excitedly as he shines his light on the stone walls and ceiling. Returning to the caves entrance, he looks at the signboard showing drawings of natives performing many of their daily activities. Although this is a very fun diversion, it is soon time to continue our journey to Ape Cave.

Starting back up the trail, I see the brilliant purple of wild Orchids among the trees undergrowth and point them out to Loren. A wonderful surprise, I can imagine the natives walking this same path and appreciating the ancestors of these flower's beauty, just as we are. Continuing our climb back up to the parking lot we are soon on the road again.

The sun is getting low in the sky
as we pull into the parking lot for
Ape Cave.
We prepare for the dampness of
the caves interior by putting on
our coats.
Testing our headlamps and
flashlights, we make sure they
are working.
Strapping on our backpacks, we
make the short walk to the trail
and are soon among the trees.

After leaving the parking lot that is still warm from the sun, the forest air feels cool against our faces.
The smell of old leaves grows stronger as we enter the woods and the sunlight is less bright.

THE FOLLOWING ARE
PROHIBITED IN APE CAVE
SMOKING
PETS
FOOD
ALCOHOL
FIRES
FIREWORKS

Reaching the Ape Cave
information boards, we read
about the history of the lava
tubes formation. It's very
interesting but we are eager
to reach the cave and continue
down the trail.

The longest lava tube known in North America
APE CAVE is a
Underground Pioneers
Build
Day 1
Day 3
Day 14
Day 100
What's in a name?
This lava tube was discovered by Lawrence Johnson in late 1951, when he nearly drove a tractor into the main entrance. Lawrence told his friend Harry Reese about his find. Harry and his three sons came early the following year and were the first known explorers of this lava tube. The Reese boys were members of the Mount St. Helens Apes, a local outdoors club, and led many visitors through the lava tube during the 1950s. This lava tube was named to honor these pioneer explorers.
As part of each tour led by the Apes, a ceremony was held to impress upon visitors that caves are special.
out, and the people sat in
the cave. After a few mome
match was lit, illuminating
the cave. In those early days
or vandalism in the cave. The
by showing people what a wild
visitors would want to help prot
Ape Cave

Soon we find ourselves looking down into the dark mouth of the cave.
Pulling his gaze from the entrance, Loren looks to me and fearfully says, "I don't think this is a good idea."
Clearly troubled by his fear of the dark, I reassure him that I will be with him the whole time.
I turn our lights on and Loren cautiously takes a step down the stairs.

Reaching the bottom of the stairs, Loren's headlamp follows his gaze as he looks around.

A lava tube formed about 2,000 years ago, we see the walls and ceiling are rounded while the floor is fairly level, but rough. Grooves in the floor run parallel to the walls, showing where the lava continued flowing after the walls and ceiling had hardened.

Loren aims his light past the nearby walls and walks in a little further.
Our lights shine only a short distance down the dark tunnel before the darkness swallows it.
This makes me wonder if he will be okay to continue.
As Loren looks around, the hesitation slowly leaves his face.
The excitement of the adventure finally overcomes his fear of the dark as he exclaims, "this is fun!"
Now confidently making his way into the cave, I follow close behind.

Cold drops of water sometimes fall from the ceiling as they add to shallow puddles on the floor. There is an unspoken rule among 5-year-olds. "A puddle of water will not be passed by without being disturbed." True to nature, Loren happily stomps his feet in the puddles. His laughter echoes in the cave as water splashes all around.

Caught up in the thrill of exploring the cave, we are surprised when we reach the end of the lava tube.

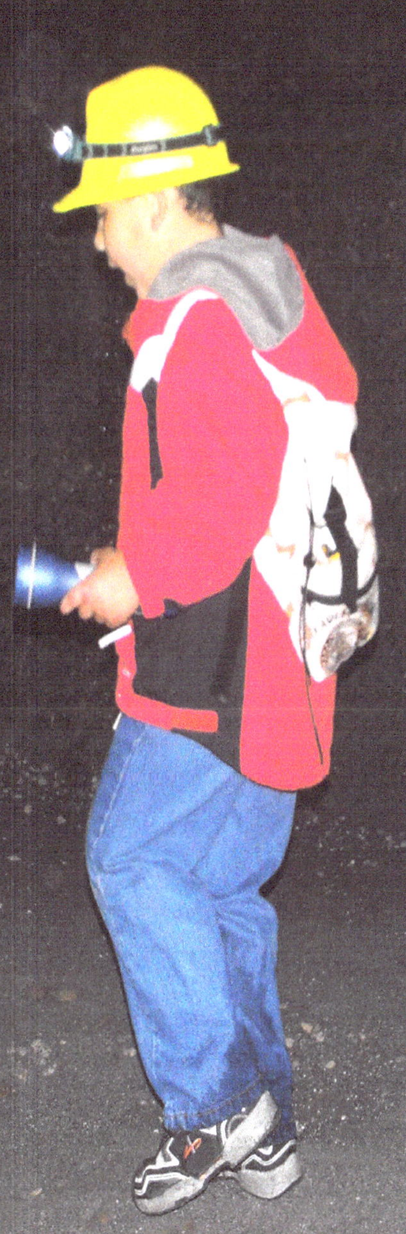

43

Loren's enthusiasm has not left
him as we retrace our steps and
make our way back to the caves
entrance.
The darkness ahead of us
lightens as we approach the
stairs, marking the end of our
adventure. The journey has
passed all too quickly, as fun
activities seem to do.
All smiles, Loren has achieved
a victory against his fear of the
dark.

The night light still glows against Loren's bedroom wall. But he will not need it to hold back his fear of the dark much longer.

The end

Loren Goes Exploring (with Dad)

The adventures we have make our time together
Pass with delight and the weight of a feather.
Seeking new experiences we're off on a whim,
We stop for supplies and are off quick again.

Taking the road that is a bit less traveled,
Delayed in our journey but plans not unraveled.
Signs by the road, "Layser cave just a mile."
We take full advantage and stop for awhile.

We see a cave that many called home,
A simple shelter, made of grey stone.
It serves to remind us all once again,
Home is any place shared with family or friend.

Light gently filters through the forest canopy,
As we ponder families living in natures harmony.
Small children running and playing in the sun,
Mothers smiling at them having great fun!

Waiting for father to return from the hunt,
Ever the slight fear his not returning to confront.
When he returns it's so good to see him,
He smiles to see their family complete again.

With no way of knowing what we leave behind,
Our love for each other we hope will leave signs.
Not a sign showing faces or the color of our hair,
But a sign that we had a great love that we shared.

So long ago we can't really say for sure,
A families love we hope through the ages endures.

Jeff Klinger